Celebrate
THE Century ®

A COLLECTION OF
COMMEMORATIVE STAMPS

1980-1989

PUT YOUR STAMP ON HISTORY
1900 ▪ 2000

![UNITED STATES POSTAL SERVICE]

UNITED STATES POSTAL SERVICE

POSTMASTER GENERAL
AND CHIEF EXECUTIVE OFFICER
William J. Henderson

SENIOR VICE PRESIDENT, GOVERNMENT
RELATIONS AND PUBLIC POLICY
Deborah K. Willhite

VICE PRESIDENT, PUBLIC AFFAIRS
AND COMMUNICATIONS
Azeezaly S. Jaffer

MANAGER, PROMOTIONS
Gary A. Thuro Jr.

PROJECT MANAGER
Clarence R. Williams

TIME-LIFE BOOKS IS A DIVISION OF TIME LIFE INC.

TIME-LIFE TRADE PUBLISHING

VICE PRESIDENT AND PUBLISHER
Neil Levin

DIRECTOR OF NEW PRODUCT DEVELOPMENT
Teresa Graham

PROJECT MANAGER
Jennifer L. Ward

PRINTING PRODUCTION MANAGER
Vanessa Hunnibell

EDITORIAL STAFF FOR CELEBRATE THE CENTURY

MANAGING EDITOR
Morin Bishop

EDITORS
John Bolster, Eve Peterson

DESIGNERS
Barbara Chilenskas, Jia Baek

WRITERS/RESEARCHERS
*Ward Calhoun, Theresa Deal,
Jeff Labrecque, Ylann Schemm*

PHOTO EDITOR
Bill Broyles

LIBRARY OF CONGRESS CATALOGING-IN-PUBLICATION DATA
Celebrate the century: a collection of commemorative stamps.
p.   cm.   Includes index.
Contents: v. 9. 1980–1989
ISBN 0-7835-5325-0
1. Commemorative postage stamps—United States—History—20th century.
2. United States—History—20th century.
I. Time-Life Books

HE6185.U5C45 1998   97–46952
769.56973—DC21   CIP

Books produced by Time-Life Trade Publishing are available at a special bulk discount for promotional and premium use. Custom adaptations can also be created to meet your specific marketing goals. Call 1-800-323-5255.

PICTURE CREDITS

Contents

Let freedom ring: The hostages returned to America in 1981 (above) and the Berlin Wall fell in 1989 (opposite).

INTRODUCTION

Given that Americans would ultimately remember the 1980s for the fall of the Berlin Wall, resurgent national pride and one of history's greatest bull markets, the decade had a strangely inauspicious beginning. Fifty-two Americans were being held hostage by Muslim extremists in Iran, the U.S. economy was caught in a stranglehold of stagflation (inflation and recession) and voters had lost faith in their president, Jimmy Carter, a Southern born-again Christian who had proffered truth-telling to heal Watergate's legacy of distrust. The decade's opening year alone contained a litany of fiascos: The FBI's Operation Abscam revealed that dozens of government and elected officials had taken cash from Arab businessmen looking for political favors; a daring mission to rescue the hostages in Iran failed miserably, leaving eight dead in the desert sand; and

the United States led a boycott of the Moscow Olympics in response to the Soviet Union's 1979 invasion of Afghanistan.

Only an incurable optimist could have believed better times were close at hand. Enter Ronald Reagan, one-time movie actor, two-time Republican governor of California. Reagan promised the country nothing less than a new era of opportunity and pride. Carter's wounded presidency was no match for the Hollywood delivery and parables of hope that Reagan—a.k.a. "the Gipper" for his appearance in the 1940 film *Knute Rockne, All American*—brought to the political table. Reagan beat Carter in a landslide, winning 489 electoral votes to the incumbent's 49. Only 11 minutes after his inauguration on January 20, 1981, the hostages who had been held in Iran for 444 days were released. While the timing suggested a show

Elliot, a sensitive child of divorce, bonded with E.T. and touched millions in Steven Spielberg's poignant, boy-meets-extraterrestrial adventure story.

of respect for the nation's new leader, the truth was that Carter had worked tirelessly at the end of his administration to negotiate the settlement.

Whether history judges him kindly or not, Ronald Reagan occupied a pivotal position in the country's stunning turnaround. A year after slashing both social spending and taxes, his supply-side reforms, later known as Reaganomics, began to take effect. From 1982 to '88, the United States enjoyed the longest peacetime economic expansion in history. There was a caveat, though. Reagan was actually *increasing* overall government spending by unprecedented amounts. With less money coming into government coffers and more going out, the United States went from being the world's biggest lender to being its biggest debtor under Reagan's watch. The largest area of government spending under Reagan was in the military. His administration allocated $2 trillion to the Pentagon in the biggest peacetime military buildup ever. Funding included research into Reagan's vision of a space-based defensive shield, dubbed Star Wars, that would shoot down incoming nuclear warheads. If

Reagan's military spending was fiscally questionable, it did help bring the Soviet Union to the bargaining table in a first step toward ending the Cold War.

Signs that Communism's grip on Eastern Europe was weakening began to appear early in the decade. In 1983 Lech Walesa, founder of Poland's Solidarity movement, was awarded the Nobel Peace Prize for his efforts in gaining workers' rights to organize. (Walesa would be elected president of Poland six years later.) In 1985 reformist Mikhail S. Gorbachev beat out hard-liners to become the General Secretary of the Soviet Union. He instituted policies of *glasnost* (openness) and *perestroika* (reform). But if Gorbachev was to successfully modernize the Soviet system, he could ill afford an escalation of the arms race. On December 8, 1987, Gorbachev and Reagan (in defiance of his more hawkish advisers) signed the Intermediate Range Nuclear Forces Treaty (INF), the first agreement to destroy nuclear missiles.

Communist regimes in Czechoslovakia, Poland and Hungary faltered after Gorbachev withdrew financial support. Reformers gained ground. In May 1989, Hungary opened its borders to the West. Other Soviet-bloc countries followed suit. On November 9, 1989, only nine months after East German leader Erich Honecker had vowed the Berlin Wall would last 100 years, that ultimate symbol of Cold War division began to crumble.

While these historic developments unfolded, the Middle East reemerged as a troubling hot spot. Terrorist attacks upon Westerners by Islamic extremists became more frequent. When a

Lebanese suicide bomber killed 241 U.S. Marines in 1983, Reagan stood tall, accepted responsibility for the massacre and reiterated his oft-repeated campaign vow *never* to negotiate with terrorists. Midway through Reagan's second term, however, the press revealed that not only was the U.S. government illegally selling military equipment to Iranian "moderates" in exchange for their help in freeing U.S. hostages in Lebanon, but that it was also diverting the proceeds of those sales to illegally arm Nicaraguan Con-

Youngsters across America perched in front of the latest electronic craze: computer video games small and affordable enough for home use.

tras in their fight against the Sandinista government. Despite the illegality of his administration's actions, Reagan himself weathered the scandal with only minor damage.

Iran-Contra was not the decade's only scandal. On October 19, 1987, Black Monday, the New York Stock Exchange plummeted 508 points (or half a trillion dollars, an amount roughly equivalent to France's GNP) and put an end to an era of rampant Wall Street speculation. Most analysts blamed the huge U.S. trade deficit and massive federal budget deficits for creating a threat of inflation and higher interest rates, two factors sure to stifle a bull market. But as with the great crash of 1929, there was another contributing element: greed. The market was full of cheaters—Michael Milken, Ivan Boesky, Dennis Levine, to name a few—who engaged in insider trading for staggering personal profit.

Reagan had been confident that an upper class with less of a tax burden would spend more money, which would "trickle down" to the middle and lower classes. In fact, with funding for social programs like food stamps and housing severely

cut, an estimated 30 million people were living below the poverty line—perhaps as many as three million of them homeless—by decade's end. The problem was exacerbated by the invention of a cheap form of cocaine called crack, which brought tremendous violence to urban streets.

But if city streets were blighted by crime and homelessness, they also witnessed the birth of hip-hop, an exuberant African-American culture comprised of equal parts rap music, break dancing and graffiti art. Albums—which were increasingly recorded on compact discs as opposed to vinyl—by rappers like Run DMC and MC Hammer quickly ascended the popular music charts. The pounding beat and inventive wordplay of hip-hop entered mainstream America at the same time that the hugely popular television series *The Cosby Show* was debunking prevailing stereotypes of the black experience. The sitcom focused not on inner-city struggles but on the dynamics of an upper-middle class family that happened to be African American. The show was a gold mine for NBC, which, along with the other networks, would soon face compe-

A thumping boom box and a flat surface provided the means to a break-dancing session on an urban street as hip-hop culture, with its catchy rhymes, flashy moves and colorful graffiti, began to take shape in the 1980s.

tition from the burgeoning cable TV industry.

While the couch potato with cable access was reveling in his vastly expanded array of viewing options, he was hit with a potential distraction: the personal computer. Once a hobbyist's obsession, the PC had revolutionized the work environment and would make inroads into home use in the '80s. Apple's Steve Jobs foresaw a day when the computer would be a common household item. Microsoft's Bill Gates hastened that day by introducing the operating system Windows and its user-friendly graphic interface. Children were among the first to benefit from the personal computer boom as schools across the United States became wired. Also thanks to the computer, kids could now play video games in an arcade, on a TV console or with a hand-held device.

In pre-Internet days, though, the PC's offerings were still relatively limited and proved no match for some of the other entertainment of the day, such as

Broadway's long-running *Cats,* Steven Spielberg's heart-tugging boy-meets-alien tale, *E.T.,* and the ever expanding appeal of the NFL, dominated in the '80s by the San Francisco 49ers, who would win four Super Bowls under the leadership of the preternaturally unflappable Joe Montana. Executing coach Bill Walsh's wide-open precision-pass offense to perfection, Montana became football's resident miracle maker, able to produce victories from seemingly hopeless situations with stunning consistency. On the opposite end of the sporting spectrum, ice dancers and figure skaters in low-cut, sequin-covered leotards brought sky-high ratings to the TV networks that covered the 1980, '84 and '88 Winter Olympics. Young and old viewers alike aspired to the grace and athleticism of Katarina Witt, Jayne Torvill and Christopher Dean and Brian Boitano.

Wide receiver Jerry Rice (No. 80) shared in two of the 49ers' four Super Bowl wins during the 1980s, a golden age for the team.

The decade also had its share of tragic heroes. On January 28, 1986, the space shuttle *Challenger* exploded in a massive fireball, killing all seven crew members, including schoolteacher Christa McAuliffe, who was to be the first ordinary citizen in space. NASA had flown 24 successful shuttle missions since it launched the shuttle program in 1981. Honoring the more than 58,000 tragic heroes of the U.S. effort in Vietnam was the Vietnam Veterans Memorial, a graceful structure that was inaugurated on November 11, 1982, on the National Mall in Washington, D.C. Five years later, 400 volunteers would spread a patchwork quilt across the same Mall to mourn loved ones who had died of AIDS, a disease that between the first case in 1981 and May 1989 claimed 56,468 lives. There was no cure in sight.

The 1980s were a complex time—both explosive and contemplative—when, from the top down, things were not necessarily as they seemed. The United States said that it would never negotiate for hostages, but did so covertly. The Berlin Wall that Honecker declared would stand for decades fell in a day. Donald Trump and Leona Helmsley built monuments to conspicuous consumption while popular musicians banded together to raise money for African famine relief. Beauty and fitness were paramount, yet people scrambled, even raised fists, to buy up homely Cabbage Patch dolls.

By decade's end, modern-day robber barons seemed to be losing ground to New Age seekers. People talked sincerely of a quieter, simpler decade to come. They would not forget the party that Wall Street had thrown, or the hangover it caused. They had experienced the emptiness that accompanies materialism and would try astrology, meditation and aromatherapy to recover their souls. They were a long way from imagining a stock market that would break the 10,000-point barrier, or a president who would nearly be felled by a 21-year-old intern.

FALL OF THE BERLIN WALL

On the evening of November 9, 1989, the Berlin Wall, the most enduring symbol of Cold War division, suspicion and hostility, began to crumble, literally and metaphorically. A wave of East Germans overwhelmed a confused border patrol and spilled into the welcoming arms of surprised West Berliners. "I just can't believe it," cried one East German. "I don't feel like I'm in prison anymore."

East and West Germans alike spontaneously began tearing at the wall with hammers, pickaxes and chisels. Together they celebrated atop the 12-foot-high structure, while East German border guards, who only hours before would have been ordered to shoot the revelers, watched in bemusement. Within 48 hours, two million East Germans visited the West, and the Berlin Wall, along with the fear and silence it inspired, was history.

Governments on both sides of the Iron Curtain were caught off guard by the events in Berlin. Just nine months earlier, Erich Honecker, leader of East Germany and the man who supervised the Wall's construction in 1961, vowed the Wall would last a hundred years. Few doubted him. Even West German chancellor Helmut Kohl scoffed at the possibility just days before the fall. "This is something that is going to take many years."

Fall of the Berlin Wall

33 USA

The Wall had become a permanent fixture in the lives of Berliners, many of whom awoke one August morning in 1961 to find their routes to work blocked by a curtain of barbed wire. East Germany, in an effort to stem mass defections to the West, erected its "anti-fascist protection wall" in a single day. Friends were divided, families separated. Over time, slabs of concrete replaced the barbed wire. Trenches, bunkers, attack dogs and sharpshooters were installed, and Berlin became a microcosm of the ideological struggle between East and West.

The Wall divided a city, a people, a continent,

East Berliners crowded atop the Berlin Wall (above) and flooded into West Berlin's Potsdamer Platz (left).

11

and to an extent—the world. When President Kennedy visited Berlin in June 1963, he stood in the shadow of the Wall and told an adoring crowd, "There are many people in the world who really don't understand, or say they don't, what is the great issue between the free world and the Communist world. *Lasst sie nach Berlin kommen* (Let them come to Berlin)."

By the time the Wall was officially completed in 1963, it ran 28 miles through the heart of the city, dissecting roads and even houses in its path. Although the Wall curtailed the flood of East German refugees, hundreds still attempted daring and often ingenious escapes to the West. Some East Berliners who lived in houses along the Wall jumped out windows onto mattresses or nets on the western side; some tried to vault over the Wall with stilts; others used the sewers and under-

ground tunnels. Two families even fled in a home-made hot-air balloon. Unfortunately, many attempts ended in tragedy. Estimates of the number of people who lost their lives trying to find their way through, around, beneath or over the Wall between 1961 and 1989 run as high as 800.

For 50 years the Soviet military had imposed order on Eastern Europe. But when Mikhail Gorbachev came to power in the Soviet Union in 1985, he introduced a series of reforms—*perestroika*—that gave hope to freedom-starved citizens of the Soviet-bloc nations. Reformers and demonstrators were emboldened when Gorbachev declared, "Any nation has the right to decide its fate by itself." Cut off from Soviet support, Communist regimes in Hungary, Czechoslovakia and Poland quickly tumbled, and in May 1989 Hungary opened its borders to the West.

West German demonstrators waved their flags at East German police (left) just before the once impassable barrier of concrete, barbed wire and guards (bottom, in 1964) gave way to openings both large (opposite) and small (inset).

"It's amazing how warmly we were greeted. We were applauded. They cried. They were just as happy as we were."

—*AN EAST GERMAN STUDENT,*
November 1989

Hundreds of thousands of East Germans flocked there en route to Western Europe, where they would seek refuge in embassies.

When other neighboring countries promised to open their borders to the West, East Germany realized the Wall had grown obsolete. Pro-democracy demonstrations were drawing crowds of 500,000. In response, the government ousted Honecker and promised reform. But the effort was too little, too late. On November 3, 1989, Czechoslovakia opened its borders to the West, and another wave of East Germans fled. In a November 9 press conference with German and foreign journalists, desperate East Berlin officials, without consulting Moscow, vaguely described a softening of travel restrictions in the hope that the exodus would cease: Citizens could apply for private trips abroad "without preconditions," and authorities would issue visas for "permanent departures" without delay.

East Berliners who heard the broadcast made their way toward the Wall to see if the claim was true. The border guards turned them away. Soon, however, the trickle of curious Berliners grew into an ocean, and the people began to chant, "Open the gate!" and "We are the people!" The panicked border patrol waited for instructions, but before receiving any, they were overwhelmed by the crowd at the Bornholmer Strasse crossing point. Within an hour, Checkpoint Charlie, the gateway to the American sector, was opened, and the celebration ensued. In the euphoria that followed, the people of Berlin switched from chanting, "We are the people!" to "We are one people!" The reunification of Germany had begun.

Some sections of the Wall were pulled down (above), some were breached with hammer and chisel (opposite, inset); no matter the method, the Wall's demise brought curious crowds (below) and jubilant celebration (opposite, at the Brandenburg Gate).

Aftermath

With the symbolic and physical dismantling of the Wall, a cry for reunification went up immediately throughout Germany. Though officials called for caution, the two Germanys became one again less than a year after the Wall disappeared entirely on October 3, 1990.

The Wall's fall foreshadowed the political decline of Mikhail Gorbachev, who survived a right-wing coup in 1991 only to lose popular support to Russian president Boris Yeltsin. In December 1991 the Union of Soviet Socialist Republics ceased to exist.

Pieces of the Wall have found their way to the United States and other countries, where they are sold as souvenirs and monuments.

E.T.: The Extra-Terrestrial

"E.T. phone home." With these innocuous words, E.T., the wrinkled extraterrestrial sage and wide-eyed innocent, entered the American consciousness. It was the summer of 1982, and director Steven Spielberg's *E.T.: The Extra-Terrestrial*, a $10.5 million "fairy tale for the '80s" had just opened in movie theaters. Its stunning craftsmanship and universally appealing story line of friendship between a lonely boy and an extraterrestrial made it one of the most beloved and lucrative films of all time, grossing $200 million during its first 66 days alone.

E.T. went on to win four Academy Awards, one for its original score (by John Williams), two for sound and one for visual effects (created by George Lucas's Industrial Light and Magic Company), as well as Golden Globes for Best Motion Picture (Drama) and Best Score.

The idea for *E.T.* came to Spielberg during the intensive *Raiders of the Lost Ark* shoot in far-off Tunisia in 1980. Spielberg channeled his homesickness into a lonely-boy-meets-alien idea, which he pitched to screenwriter Melissa Mathison, who was on the set with her future husband, Harrison Ford. Mathison—who had also written the screenplay for *The Black Stallion*, a children's classic—responded several months later with a beautifully constructed fable about a depressed boy named Elliot whose father had walked out on the family. The lad discovers and befriends a stranded space alien, who quickly establishes a telepathic bond with him. Hilarious interspecies shenanigans ensue, and despite governmental pursuit, Elliot, with the help of newfound friends, manages to safely return his otherworldly companion to the mother ship.

E.T. and Elliot (above) teamed up to outrun the authorities (left) and capture moviegoers' affections.

Spielberg's own childhood experience of constant relocation and painful disorientation provided him with ample insight into the story. "Just when I would find a best friend, at the moment of my greatest comfort and tranquillity, we'd go somewhere else. The older I got, the harder it got. *E.T.* reflects a lot of that. When Elliot finds E.T., he hangs on. He announces in no uncertain terms, 'I'm keeping him,' and he means it."

Choosing the right boy to play Elliot was crucial to the film's effectiveness. Hundreds of kids auditioned for the part before a nine-year-old from San Antonio, Henry Thomas, was chosen for his strong and serious presence. Thomas won rave reviews from film critics such as Roger Ebert, who credited him with "the best little-boy performance I've ever seen in an American film."

Finding the right E.T. proved far more difficult. Months of designing and deliberating produced a frustratingly worthless $700,000 prototype. "I wanted a creature only a mother could love," Spielberg said. He finally found his answer in a design by Carlo Rambaldi. The artist and special effects designer had won two Academy Awards for his work on *King Kong* and *Alien* and easily captured E.T.'s blend of aged wisdom and comic innocence. (He modeled the extraterrestrial's irresistible mug on the faces of Albert Einstein and poet Carl Sandburg.) Rambaldi's team

"*E.T.: The Extra-Terrestrial* is a movie, like *The Wizard of Oz*, that you can grow up with and grow old with, and it won't let you down."

—*Roger Ebert, film critic, 1982*

Alien adventures: E.T. flees in Elliot's bicycle basket (opposite), earns a kiss from Elliot's little sister, Gertie (above, played by Drew Barrymore), plays dress-up (below) and masters electronic games while Elliot is at school (right).

spent six months and $1.5 million working around the clock to create three separate models capable of handling E.T's complex tasks. An electronic E.T. provided endearing facial expressions—rolling eyes, lifted eyebrows and a nose that wrinkled on cue—for closeups. The mechanical E.T., bolted to the floor and manipulated by 12 operators using control panels attached to 20-foot cables, produced E.T.'s raspy, desperate wheezing (air was slowly squeezed in and out of plastic bags) and his famous beating and glowing heart. The "walking" E.T. costume had a waddling Donald Duck derrière and was alternately worn by two dwarves and a little boy born without legs. All three E.T. models stood just 3 feet 6

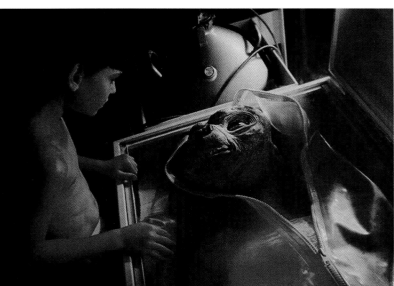

inches and had skeletons of aluminum and steel. The exterior of fiberglass, foam rubber and polyurethane created a veritable steam bath for the three E.T. "walkers." A professional mime donned "E.T. gloves" for the more nuanced hand movements, when E.T. touches Elliot, for example, or reaches for a piece of candy. When, on her first day of shooting, the mime's hands shook from a surfeit of coffee, a quintessential E.T. trait was born. As Spielberg decided, E.T. was, after all, new to earth and tentatively exploring everything for the first time.

E.T.'s unusual voice was created after the sound designer overheard a 65-year-old retired speech teacher talking to a salesclerk. Her two-pack-a-day cigarette rasp—coupled with her absence of dentures—produced E.T.'s memorable voice. An otter's shriek doubled as his scream and a crewman's burp provided the little guy's memorable beer belch.

Some viewers have found all manner of alle-

When E.T. is discovered by federal officials, Elliot's house is quarantined (opposite, top) and E.T., who falls fatally ill, is brought back to life by his love for Elliot (opposite, bottom). After tearful good-byes (inset), E.T. boards his mother ship (left).

gorical subtexts running through *E.T.*, but most have simply loved this surprisingly poignant feel-good movie for its face value. Spielberg's ability to express wonder and hope and communicate a child's point of view has turned E.T. into a beloved icon of '80s popular culture. As film critic Andrew Sarris put it, "E.T. is the teddy bear we crush forever to our bleeding hearts. E.T. is every childish fantasy we never outgrew. E.T. is the eternal child in all of us."

Aftermath

By the end of the 1980s *E.T.* had generated more than $1 billion at movie theaters and $400 million in video sales. Merchandising of T-shirts, video games, bubblegum cards, lunchboxes, pajamas, books and dolls, to name a few items, added to *E.T.* mania. Seventeen years after it debuted in theaters, *E.T.* was considered a classic, and Spielberg had become one of the most influential directors in the last quarter of the twentieth century.

FIGURE SKATING

From the moment the Winter Olympics came to television in the 1960s, figure skating, with its unique combination of athletic skill and balletic grace, earned the highest viewership numbers of the Winter Games. Not bad for a sport some critics have never considered legitimate.

Sport or artistic performance, it mattered little to the millions who became lifelong fans while watching perky Connecticut-native Dorothy Hamill win the gold medal in her homemade pink dress at the 1976 Games in Innsbruck. Girls everywhere bought ice skates and adopted Hamill's signature wedge hair style. It was the last time, though, that a single skater would own the spotlight.

By the early 1980s a new class of talented and charismatic skaters lifted figure skating's profile higher still. Gone were the unadorned, high-necked skating dresses of the '70s; in came low-cut, sequin-covered leotards for women and bared chests for men. Hamill left Olympic competition for the professional circuit, and three skating princesses—Linda Fratianne, Elaine Zayak and Rosalynn Sumners—reigned over the rinks. Sumners captivated audiences with her elegant twirls and leg extensions while Fratianne and Zayak brought jumping to the fore.

One of the first females to regularly use triple jumps in competition, Fratianne set in motion competitive figure skating's shift from an exhibition of artistry to one of jumping prowess. Triple jumps became Zayak's trademark at the '82 world championships, where she landed a record six triples dur-

The duo Torvill and Dean of England (left) and Hamilton of the U.S. (above) both skated to gold in Sarajevo.

"I felt I let down the whole U.S. But then I got so many letters of support, I realized it really didn't matter that much that I didn't win the gold. Katarina is a beautiful girl, a warm person, and I'm happy for her."

—DEBI THOMAS, former Olympic skater, after her loss to East Germany's Katarina Witt

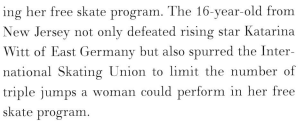

The team of Gordeeva and Grinkov (left) lit up the ice at the 1989 world championships in Paris. At the Calgary Olympics in 1988 Witt (opposite, below) and Thomas (below) both skated to *Carmen* as Witt took the gold and Thomas the bronze.

ing her free skate program. The 16-year-old from New Jersey not only defeated rising star Katarina Witt of East Germany but also spurred the International Skating Union to limit the number of triple jumps a woman could perform in her free skate program.

Zayak, Sumners and Witt met at the '84 Olympics in Sarajevo. Witt's shapely figure and sweet-yet-sexy grin charmed the world, judges included, and she upset Sumners for the gold (Zayak finished sixth). The victory solidified her standing as an international star. The men's singles competition was just as thrilling. Solid jumper and able showman Scott Hamilton followed up his fifth-place finish at Lake Placid in 1980 with a gold in the men's singles, the first for an American man since 1960.

In Sarajevo the British ice-dancing duo of Jayne Torvill and Christopher Dean won nine perfect scores from the judges for their interpretation of Ravel's *Bolero*. The mesmerizing performance, which easily won the gold medal, now resides in the pantheon of great skating routines—the pair estimated they performed it nearly 2,000 times before the end of the century. Still, the 1980's competitive pinnacle lay four years away.

Two rivalries emerged at the 1988 Winter Olympics in Calgary. The first, between Witt and American Debi Thomas, a 20-year-old Stanford pre-med student, was dubbed the "Battle of the Carmens" due to their identical—and coincidental—choice of music. *Newsweek* wrote of the rivalry, "In all of figure skating's echoes of ballet or Hollywood through the years, no duel ever encompassed the head-to-head drama of Thomas against Witt."

The 22-year-old Witt, who trailed Thomas after the short program, excelled in artistic interpretation and theatrical performance; Thomas in athleticism. While Witt flirted with the crowd

and omitted difficult jumps, the daredevil jumper Thomas fell on a triple toe loop combination and narrowly avoided a second spill by catching the ice with her hand. Witt prevailed. The gold made her the first woman in more than 50 years to win two gold medals in Olympic singles competition. Thomas, the first African American to medal in the Winter Games, took home the bronze. Their competition was a highlight of the Games and further increased the popularity of the sport.

On the men's side the competition was christened "The Battle of the Brians," after its participants, Brian Boitano of the United States and Brian Orser of Canada. Boitano, whose soaring triple axels and Lutzes prompted Hamilton to call him the best jumper in history, had polished the artistic side of his performance enough to win the gold; Orser, the local favorite, took the silver medal.

While the Brians battled it out, the Russian pairs team of Ekaterina Gordeeva and Sergei Grinkov infused Calgary's ice rink with love and romance. Their polished skating—they seemed to move as one—and arresting good looks seduced audiences and earned them the gold. During their career, they would win two gold medals, four world championships and each other's hearts (they married in 1991).

Figure skating's dream team—Boitano, Orser, Witt and Thomas—retired from competitive skating following the 1988 world championships in Budapest. The next wave of skaters—led by Kurt Browning, a 21-year-old from Canada who landed the first quadruple jump in competition, and Kristi Yamaguchi of the United States, who would win an Olympic gold and two world championships—proved to be worthy heirs. Call it sport or performance, figure skating is sure to mesmerize audiences with its spins and lifts and jumps for a long time to come.

Aftermath

After retiring, most of the skating stars of the 1980s entered the professional realm of all-star exhibitions and ice-show tours. Their impact was felt into the late '90s, however, as figure skating continued to gain in popularity. In 1998, TV ratings for figure skating events at the Winter Olympics surpassed those for the World Series.

The sport took an unsavory twist shortly before the 1994 Olympics when one of the gold-medal favorites, Nancy Kerrigan of the United States, was attacked and clubbed above her right knee after a practice. She missed the Olympic qualifying competition at the U.S. nationals as a result of her injuries, but in view of the extraordinary circumstances, the U.S. Figure Skating Association (USFSA) allowed her to join the eventual U.S. champion, Tonya Harding, at the Games. Harding, who denied involvement in the attack, later admitted that she had known after the assault that members of her entourage were behind it. Kerrigan won the silver at the Games, finishing second to 16-year-old Oksana Baiul of Ukraine. Harding faltered and finished eighth and was later stripped of her national title and forced to resign from the USFSA.

Gordeeva and Grinkov won another gold in '94, but their career was tragically cut short in '95 when Grinkov died suddenly of a heart attack. Gordeeva resumed her career in 1996.

The darlings of the late '90s circuit were Tara Lipinski and Michelle Kwan of the U.S., who won gold and silver, respectively, at the '98 Games in Nagano.

PERSONAL COMPUTERS

The "information revolution" that futurists have long predicted has arrived, bringing with it the promise of dramatic changes in the way people live and work, perhaps even in the way they think. America will never be the same. —TIME, 1983

Time's sensational prediction of the transformative powers of the personal computer—a computer small enough and inexpensive enough for individual owner- ship—proved to be not overstated but, in fact, conservative. The 1982 "Machine of the Year," as *Time* named it, not only changed America, it also changed the world.

One of the first affordable personal computers was the Altair 8800, the creation of MITS, a foundering calculator company based in Albu- querque. Featured on the cover of *Popular Elec- tronics* in January 1975, the almost useless machine—it lacked both a keyboard and a screen—helped spawn two of the PC industry's biggest players: Apple Computer and Microsoft.

As a young computer hobbyist in the heart of northern California's Silicon Valley, Stephen (Woz) Wozniak tinkered with his Altair 8800. He and boyhood friend Steve Jobs had built prim- itive computers, called "blue boxes," to tap into phone lines and place long-distance calls for free from the Jobs family garage. When Woz built his own com- puter and called it—at Jobs's suggestion—the Apple I, the pair was on its way to making history, along with a sizable fortune. Their goal was to make user-friendly computers, and with $90,000 in financing from retired Intel millionaire Mike Markkula, the two Steves released the Apple II in March 1977, naming their company after

By the end of the decade PCs had begun to change the look of offices (left) and classrooms (above).

> **"The real purpose of learning how computers work should be to improve human logic and thought processes, to make people more creative, not simply more dependent on machines."**
>
> —*SEYMOUR PAPERT, MIT professor, in* **Forbes** *magazine, 1983*

their product. Within a year Apple Computer had logged $7 million in sales.

But for a computer to be useful, it must be able to perform more than just rudimentary functions. Enter Harvard sophomore Bill Gates and his Altair 8800. Gates was so inspired by the possibilities for personal computer software development that he left school after creating a programming system for the Altair along with his friend Paul Allen. In February 1975, after six weeks of work on their product, they licensed it to MITS on a royalty basis. This turned out to be a shrewd move, and the beginning of the revolution.

In 1980 Apple's sales approached the $100-million mark, and when the company's stock went public that year, Wozniak and Jobs became instant multimillionaires. Corporate monolith IBM joined the fray in August 1981 with its IBM PC, which was equipped with the MS-DOS operating system, a program developed by the company Gates and Allen recently founded, Microsoft. MS-DOS linked the hardware and software.

The IBM PC was standard equipment in the business world by '82, and when IBM disclosed the PC's operational details, the number of PC manufacturers exploded. Houston-based Compaq produced the first "clone" in 1982; an estimated 150 more followed. Because Microsoft retained the right to license MS-DOS to other manufacturers, the new "clones" benefited from the same

From grade school (opposite) to college (above), students were among the first to benefit from the PC explosion that would eventually make desktop IBMs (inset, left) and Macintoshes (inset, far left) as familiar as household appliances.

operating programs as the IBM PC. By the end of that year, three million PCs had been sold for a total of more than $5 billion.

The buying frenzy didn't last, however. New Apple and IBM models languished in the stores in 1983 largely due to overbuying by retail stores and the limited number of software programs on the market. Microsoft, on the other hand, flour-ished. It sold half a million copies of MS-DOS and released Microsoft Word, a word processing software program, in November '83.

Meanwhile, Apple was busy planning its next model, the Macintosh. The new computer would feature a "graphical user interface," a technology developed at Xerox in the early '70s that used pic-tures to represent functions. Xerox, however, was

Visionary Steve Jobs (top) and business whiz Bill Gates (above) were the two people most responsible for making the personal computer the ideal complement to home (right) and school life (opposite, top and bottom).

slow to market the technology. Apple's Steve Jobs was not. He envisioned the Macintosh as the next home appliance and targeted a huge, virtually untapped market: Only two percent of U.S. households owned computers at the time.

A television commercial that aired only once, during the '84 Super Bowl, announced, "On January 23, Apple will introduce the Macintosh and you'll see why 1984 won't be 1984." What users of the computer later saw was a screen that simulated a real desktop with files represented by pictures or "icons." A hand-controlled "mouse" allowed users to bypass the cumbersome task of entering hard-to-remember commands via the keyboard.

After an initial surge, sales tapered off. Apple CEO John Sculley decided that he had been blinded by Jobs's idea. "People weren't about to buy $2,000-

Aftermath

By the mid-1990s nearly 90 percent of the world's PCs were IBMs or IBM clones; Microsoft dominated the operating-system market; and personal computers could be found in approximately 40 percent of all U.S. households. Microsoft's Windows program made Macintosh computers largely indistinguishable from IBM and its clones until Apple introduced the iMac in 1998 and injected the market with much-needed product differentiation. The monitor-and-computer-in-one was contructed with clear and candy-colored plastic. Its speed and memory were formidable.

Steve Jobs's vision of the PC as a home appliance was realized with the explosion of the Internet in the mid-'90s. Initially devoted to spreadsheet programs and video games, the personal computer has evolved into a tool for everything from designing books to shopping for a mortgage and participating in auctions.

In 1999 Microsoft chairman Bill Gates possessed a personal fortune estimated at $85 billion, more than the gross domestic product of the Philippines.

computers to play a video game, balance a checkbook or file gourmet recipes," he said. "The average consumer simply couldn't do something useful with a computer." As for sales in the business world, the Macintosh was hampered by its insufficient memory and lack of speed. The publishing and educational realms, however, latched onto the "Mac" for its desktop publishing capabilities and ease of use. Despite this niche, financial problems and managerial conflicts resulted in the departure of Wozniak in February 1985. Jobs followed seven months later.

Convinced that Macintosh had hit upon an essential truth—that user-friendly software would be crucial to reviving computer sales and making the

PC indispensable at the office and home—Microsoft set out to create a new operating system. The first version of Microsoft's Windows was released in October 1985. It employed the graphical user interface and gradually won over PC users.

By the end of the decade, Microsoft was the largest software maker in the world, with annual profits of more than $170 million, and Gates's personal fortune was estimated at $3 billion. Personal computers accounted for 40 percent of all computer sales. But the profit PCs generated is only half the story. The other half is that they transformed the way people work, the way people live and perhaps even the way people think.

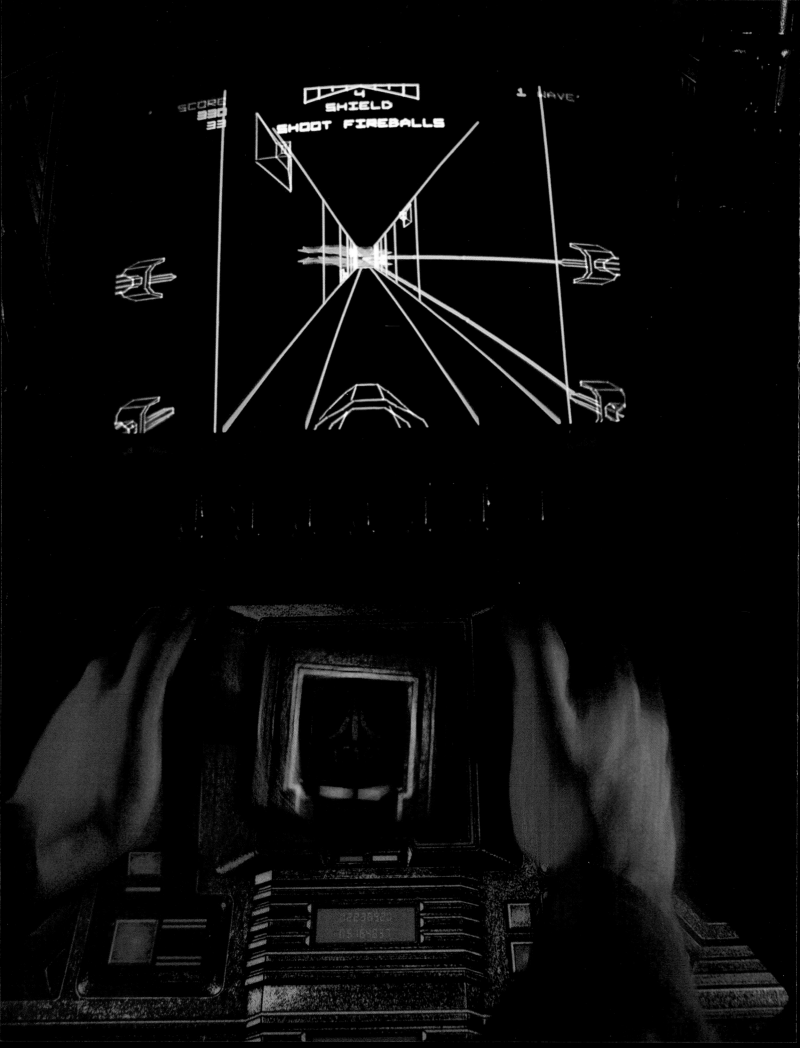

VIDEO GAMES

If there were a video game based on the short but eventful history of video games, it would begin in slow motion, then rapidly accelerate to warp speed. Players would have to adapt to mercurial changes in format, and the game would twice spring back to life after the GAME OVER icon had flashed onscreen and the machine had gone silent.

Such a game would be no more bewildering than some of the current offerings of Nintendo, Sega and Sony. Indeed, video games have come a long way since they first emerged from the primordial cyber-soup in 1962. That's when an electrical engineering student named Steve Russell created *Spacewar* on a mainframe computer at MIT. But since computers were bigger than walk-in fridges in those days, and they had price tags to match, *Spacewar* did not exactly kick-start the video-game craze. In fact, it never escaped university engineering departments. Computers

would have to speed up and slim down before video games could enter the mainstream.

That process would take a decade, and when it was complete, the game that led the way was not Russell's battling-spaceships concoction but the decidedly more genteel *Pong*. A crudely rendered game of tennis with two white bars as electronic racquets, *Pong* is to *Mortal Kombat*, the popular 1990s game, what Etch-A-Sketch drawings are to the Sistine Chapel. Yet *Pong* single-handedly launched the industry in 1972, taking arcades and bars by storm.

A home version of the game appeared in 1974, and in '76, Atari, the company behind *Pong*, was sold to Warner Bros. for $28 million. Video games had arrived. But they would not stay long. At the end of '76, the market crashed under the weight of a thousand *Pong* knockoffs. Bored by the indistinguishable offerings, consumers stopped buying. The dozens of knockoff manufacturers faded as

Kids spent hours and countless quarters (above) in front of games like Atari Computer Video Arcade (left).

First came *Pong* (opposite, bottom), then *Pac-Man* (inset, far right), then *Punch-out* (inset, right); a game expo attendee in New York learned how to battle asteroids (above) while roller skaters in California took time out from the rink to play (opposite, top).

quickly as they had arrived. Only Atari, with Warner's backing, survived.

Atari rebounded with *Breakout*, while Midway Games launched *Space Invaders* and Namco set *Pac-Man* a-gobbling. They resuscitated the industry and ushered in the golden age of video games. Both the arcade and home-console markets flourished in the early 1980s. Teeming with adolescent boys, the arcade became a fixture in malls across the country.

Home-console games now had cartridges—an Atari innovation—so that instead of buying, say, a *Breakout* console, consumers bought a system and plugged any number of different games into it.

The boom was in full swing again. Mattel launched Intellivision in 1980, and Coleco flicked the switch on Colecovision in '82. *Pac-Man* became the most popular arcade game of all time, with 300,000 units worldwide and an equal

"*Defender* was my first game, back in 1980, and it was just me and a couple of other guys programming it. These days when we do a video game it's almost like a Hollywood team. We have a guy just writing musical scores for the game, four or five guys doing the artwork, and three or four programmers. It's a huge, huge thing."

—*Eugene Jarvis, video game designer, 1996*

number of imitation machines. Newcomers seized some of Atari's market share, but the pioneer maintained its supremacy and broke all sales records by licensing *Space Invaders* for home use. The arcade version of *Space Invaders,* with its inexorable rows of alien attackers, was so popular it caused a coin shortage in Japan in 1978 and '79.

Arcade video games gulped down 20 billion quarters—five billion dollars—in 1981. The home-console market was worth another billion. Together they generated more revenue than the U.S. movie and Nevada gambling industries combined. And then, once more, the bubble burst. Imitation cartridges glutted the home market, causing confusion and ultimately blunting consumer inter-

est. Arcade managers, disenchanted with the juvenile-delinquent reputations of their customers, left the business. In 1984 Warner Bros. disbanded Atari, and Mattel gave up on electronics. The market was in a deep freeze throughout 1985.

Enter Nintendo of Japan, which brought its Nintendo Entertainment System (NES) to the U.S. in 1986. The star of NES was the unlikely, mustachioed plumber, Mario, from the game *Super Mario Bros.* Mario chases a gorilla over outlandish pitfalls in an effort to rescue the beast's captive, Princess Toadstool. While he was at it, he rescued the home video game market—and made the U.S. safe for Nintendo competitors Sega and, later, Sony PlayStation. The game was back on.

Aftermath

Nintendo, Sony and Sega have dominated the video game market in the 1990s, improving the depth, realism and complexity of their games with each passing year.

The arcade business never recovered from its early '80s collapse, but arcade-style cabinet games continue to thrive in single units or small groups in pizza shops, 7-11s and the like.

Licensing of video game spinoff products ranging from feature films to T-shirts, hats, mugs and action figures has helped expand and sustain the industry, which reattained multibillion-dollar revenue levels in the mid-'90s.

A group of boys took on *Defender* (opposite) while a lone player puzzled over *Q*bert* (top); Nintendo's vast offerings in home video software (above) breathed new life into the game market in the late '80s.

VIETNAM VETERANS MEMORIAL

The ambivalence Americans felt, and still feel, about the Vietnam War made the return home a bitter experience for many veterans of that conflict. Unlike their fathers, who were welcomed home with ticker-tape parades and celebrated as heroes after World War II, this generation of vets felt rejected, even guilty, as if its sacrifices were not honorable patriotic duty but misdeeds best ignored or forgotten. As if they, the soldiers, might be responsible for dividing the American public so bitterly.

The idea then of commemorating those who served and lost their lives in Vietnam with a memorial was not obvious, even to veterans. In March 1979, more than five years after the cease fire, infantryman Jan Scruggs, a Vietnam veteran who had gone straight from high school to the army, went with his wife to see *The Deer Hunter*, a movie about three close friends from Pennsylvania who are captured while serving in Vietnam and endure

atrocities as prisoners of war. Scruggs, who served in an infantry company that suffered terrible casualties—half of the men were killed or wounded badly enough to be evacuated—returned home from the movie devastated. He had been among the wounded in Vietnam and had witnessed the suffering and sacrifice of fellow servicemen.

Scruggs sat up into the early hours of the morning after seeing the movie, reliving his combat experiences, witnessing again the deaths of friends, and the idea of a memorial came to him. That morning he told his wife, "I'm going to build a memorial to all the guys who served in Vietnam."

Scruggs moved quickly. Teaming up with lawyer and air force veteran Bob Doubek, he founded the Vietnam Veterans Memorial Fund the following month and began soliciting private contributions to pay for the project. In 1980 the Senate approved a bill to provide a site on the

Flowers were placed at the Wall (left) in memory of the more than 58,000 soldiers whose names are etched on its face (above).

"The Wall is designed for you, for everyone, to come and bring their thoughts and emotions to the Wall. You make it come alive, and I want to thank you for your service to this country."

—Maya Lin, designer of the Wall, at the Tenth Annual Commemoration Ceremony, 1992

National Mall in Washington, D.C., for the memorial. And on November 11, 1982, during the five-day National Salute to Vietnam Veterans that drew thousands of people, military and civilian alike, the Vietnam Veterans Memorial was dedicated.

Rather than handpicking a famous architect or sculptor to design the memorial, Scruggs's group organized a design competition that turned out to be among the biggest, most democratic competitions ever held in the United States. Citizens were issued an open invitation to participate, and a total of 1,421 designs were submitted and dis-

played in a giant government aircraft hangar in a Washington suburb. On April 27, 1981, an eight-person panel of architects, landscape architects, sculptors and a design critic chosen by the Memorial Fund gathered to begin the selection process. Five days later, they had their winner: 21-year-old Maya Lin, an undergraduate majoring in architecture at Yale University.

Lin's winning design was simplicity itself. The memorial she envisioned and eventually built was composed of two triangular sections of highly polished black granite set together in a wide angle. One section of the Wall was aligned with the Lincoln Memorial, some 600 feet away, the other with the Washington Monument. Unlike those two towering structures, however, Lin's monument sliced into the earth, leaving the tops of the walls at ground level on one side. Visitors walked down a gently sloping path paralleling the polished face of the monument, on which were carved the names of the Vietnam War's more than 58,000 dead or missing American soldiers. Lin arranged the names chronologically, rather than alphabetically, beginning with the first fatality in 1959 and ending with the last in 1975, when Communist forces finally defeated South Vietnam. Lin had been moved when, during her first two years at Yale, the names of alumni killed in Vietnam were added to a campus memorial that held the names of alumni who had died in earlier wars.

The choice of Lin's design was not without controversy. Heroic monuments of gleaming white marble are the norm in Washington, and many people, including numerous Vietnam vets and politicians, thought that Lin's restrained, abstract design was inappropriate. Opponents labeled it "a tombstone," "a degrading ditch," or

Some visitors brought mementos to the Wall, such as combat boots (left) or a photograph and a medal (opposite), while others took away rubbings (inset, above). Almost all were touched by the Wall's stark simplicity as it stretched toward the Washington Monument (above).

43

Touching the names on the Vietnam Veterans Memorial brought solace to visitors (left, top and bottom) as did leaving tributes (above); every day, thousands of people walk along the granite Wall (opposite) designed by Maya Lin (inset, opposite), then a 21-year-old architecture student.

"a black gash of shame and sorrow." In the face of mounting controversy, Secretary of the Interior James Watt refused to permit groundbreaking unless the design was modified.

Scruggs's group resolved the conflict by proposing to erect a statue in the heroic tradition, along with a flagpole, at the head of the footpath that would run through the Memorial. The statue, by sculptor Frederick E. Hart, would be composed of three slightly larger-than-life, weary-looking infantrymen, one black and two white, and would bear the emblems of the five services that fought in Vietnam—the army, air force, navy, marines and Coast Guard. The statue was dedicated on November 10, 1984, two years after the Wall's dedication.

With both the Hart and Lin memorials in place, the country could continue its work of healing the public and private wounds that the war had inflicted upon it.

Aftermath

Despite the controversy that clouded its early days, the Wall soon became by far the most popular memorial in Washington, with two to three million visitors a year. Many tributes to veterans are left at the Wall, including letters, obituaries, articles of clothing, photographs, a POW/MIA bracelet, a Purple Heart medal and a high-school varsity letter. All the mementos—some 50,000 through 1999—are collected and stored in a government warehouse. Since the Wall's dedication in 1982, dozens of memorials honoring Vietnam vets have been built around the country. On Veteran's Day, 1993, a statue honoring the 11,000 women who served in the war was erected near the Wall.

45

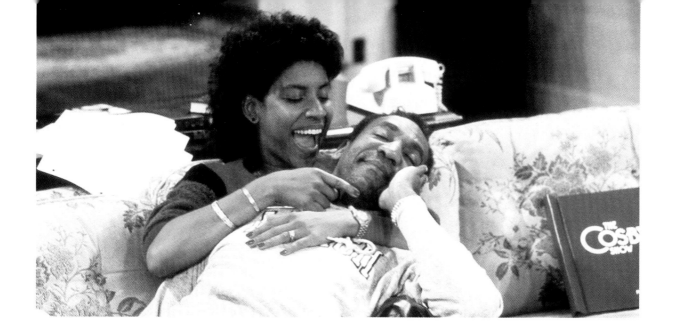

THE COSBY SHOW

"I just hope they get out of the house before we die," sighed Bill Cosby's character, Dr. Heathcliff Huxtable, at the end of the premiere episode of *The Cosby Show*. The doctor was speaking of his children and his desire to one day relinquish his role as family referee. Well, not so soon. The Huxtables of Brooklyn, New York, captured the interest of TV viewers across America, and their show quickly became the most popular situation comedy on television. They would stay together under one roof for a long time to come.

The Cosby Show debuted on September 20, 1984, a time when some television critics were proclaiming the situation comedy passé. Cosby, who began his career as a groundbreaking stand-up comedian, was already a veteran TV performer. He was one of the first African-American actors to star on a network drama when, as undercover agent Alexander

Scott on *I Spy*, he won three Emmy Awards from 1965 to '68. He later hosted and did character voices for the popular '70s Saturday-morning cartoon *Fat Albert and the Cosby Kids*. But these considerable accomplishments were a mere prelude to the success he would achieve on the eponymous show he co-created with Ed Weinberger, Michael Leeson and former ABC programming executives Marcy Carsey and Tom Werner.

While the premise for *The Cosby Show* was simple—an affluent married couple raising five kids in a Brooklyn brownstone—it was relatively uncharted terrain for a vehicle driven by African-American stars. Earlier comedies, such as *Sanford and Son, Good Times* and *What's Happening!*, relied heavily on social stereotypes of the "black experience"—inner city settings and financial struggles—for their humor. By making Cliff an obstetrician and his

The comic duo of Phylicia Rashad and Bill Cosby (above) headed the fun-loving Huxtable family (left).

Cosby's early ventures in television included *I Spy* (left, with Robert Culp), for which he won three Emmys, and *Fat Albert and the Cosby Kids* (above). In a house domi- nated by women (oppo- site, below), Cosby's Dr. Huxtable, his son and son-in-law take on dis- tinctly female profiles to do the "pregnant dance" (opposite, above).

wife, Clair, an attorney, the show immediately challenged that precedent. While many applauded *The Cosby Show*'s approach as "refreshing," some felt it ignored the hot-button topics of race and class that affected so many African Americans.

When it was first pitched, *The Cosby Show* was simply another comedy featuring a blue-collar worker and his family; both ABC and NBC turned it down. Cosby's wife, Camille, reportedly told her husband to change the married couple to upscale professionals. The program was again rejected by ABC, but this time NBC picked it up.

Starring opposite Cosby as his wife, Clair, was Phylicia Ayers-Allen (later Phylicia Rashad). The couple had five children (four in the house and the oldest away at college): Princeton student Sondra (Sabrina Le Beauf), teenager Denise (Lisa

Bonet), eight-year-old Vanessa (Tempestt Bled-soe), "baby" Rudy (Keshia Knight Pulliam) and 14-year-old son Theo (Malcolm-Jamal Warner). Story lines focused less on the Huxtable's social standing than on the observations on family life and children that were a mainstay of Cosby's stand-up routines. Indeed, the family dynamic of the show closely mirrored Cosby's own family: He and Camille are college-educated, successful and raised five children (four girls and one boy).

Many of the sitcom's funniest moments revolved around Cliff and Theo as the only men in a house full of women. Another surefire comic staple pitted the kids against the parents in bat-tles of wit, which, when the dust settled and the lessons were learned, Cliff and Clair usually won. Whatever the setup, the payoff was audience

"I got tired of seeing TV shows that consist of a car crash, a gunman and a hooker talking to a black pimp. It was cheaper to do a series than throw out my family's six TV sets."

—BILL COSBY

laughter and soaring popularity for the show.

Halfway through its first season *The Cosby Show* was earning the highest ratings in television history. It finished third in the year-end Nielsen ratings and won the Emmy Award for Best Comedy. The following season, 1985–86, the program ranked number one and remained on top through the 1988–89 season. As it grew in popularity, new characters appeared: Cliff's and Clair's parents, Sondra's husband, Elvin, and an endless parade of friends. Famous musicians such as B.B. King, Dizzy Gillespie and Stevie Wonder popped in for cameos, reflecting Cosby's well-documented love of music.

During its prime, between 1984 and '91, *The Cosby Show* never fell below No. 5 in the Nielsens and anchored NBC's dominant Thursday night

Ignoring gender stereotypes, Cosby frequently did the cooking (opposite, above) and serving (right) in the Huxtable house, where laughter (below) and friendly competition (opposite, below) were staples.

lineup. In 1988, while the show was at its peak, its distributor, Viacom, sold the rerun rights to local stations for a staggering $500 million—quite a windfall for Viacom as well as principals Cosby, Carsey and Werner. *The Cosby Show* was the biggest thing to hit television in years. No wonder NBC chairman Grant Tinker described Cosby as "an absolute giant" in television. A giant for sure, but a gentle one whose sympathetic interaction with children always kept viewers coming back for more.

By the end of the '80s *The Cosby Show* had helped change the way African Americans are depicted on television and paved the way for a whole new crop of family-themed comedies such as *The Wonder Years, Roseanne* and *Home*

Aftermath

In the fall of 1987 *The Cosby Show* spawned its only spinoff, *A Different World,* which chronicled Denise Huxtable's college experience.

The final first-run episode of *The Cosby Show* aired on April 30, 1992, and focused on Theo's graduation from college. The show finished its last season with its lowest—but still respectable—Nielsen ranking of 15.

Bill Cosby returned to television comedy in 1996 with *Cosby* (CBS), in which he played Hilton Lucas, a victim of corporate downsizing who lives with his family in Queens, New York. Phylicia Rashad again played his wife, this time named Ruth. The show began its fourth season in the fall of 1999 but had yet to capture anywhere near the same viewership as *The Cosby Show* in the '80s.

Improvement. There were more sitcoms on prime-time TV than ever before, and *Cosby* had cemented its place as one of the most successful and influential shows in television history. For situation comedies and the audiences that love them, it's a mighty good thing that Cliff Huxtable's opening-episode prayers for a peaceful, empty nest went unanswered.

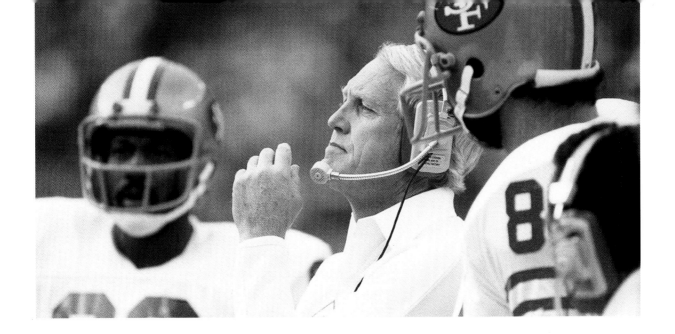

SAN FRANCISCO 49ERS

San Francisco, that picturesque city in northern California, has been identified with a great many things over the years—the majestic Golden Gate Bridge, trolley cars that climb and descend its hilly streets and destructive earthquakes, to name a few. But in the 1980s, the City by the Bay gained a new distinction as the home of one of pro football's most successful franchises ever.

The rise of the 49ers began in January 1979 with the arrival of cerebral head coach Bill Walsh, who inherited a team that had gone 2–14 the previous season and showed little potential for the type of ultraefficient, short-passing offense he envisioned. In his first full season as coach the team duplicated its abysmal 2–14 record of the previous year. The following season, after Walsh strengthened the team through the college draft, taking players he deemed suited to his West Coast offense, the 'Nin-

ers improved slightly, finishing 6–10. It was in 1981 that the team made its quantum leap: San Francisco stunned the NFL by finishing with a league-best 13–3 record to become the first team in 34 years to jump from the NFL cellar to its penthouse in a three-year span.

The 'Niners' breakthrough season was spearheaded by quarterback Joe Montana, who was in his first full year as a starter. Despite an impressive record of comeback victories during his college career at Notre Dame, Montana wasn't picked until the third round of the 1979 draft. He quickly proved to be a big-game player. In the NFC divisional playoffs after the 1981 season he threw touchdown passes of eight yards to tight end Charle Young and 58 yards to wide receiver Freddie Solomon as San Francisco dismissed the New York Giants 38–24. That victory set the stage for the NFC title game against the perennial powerhouse Dallas Cowboys.

With Montana (left) running the offense and Walsh (above) on the sidelines, the 49ers were a force to be reckoned with.

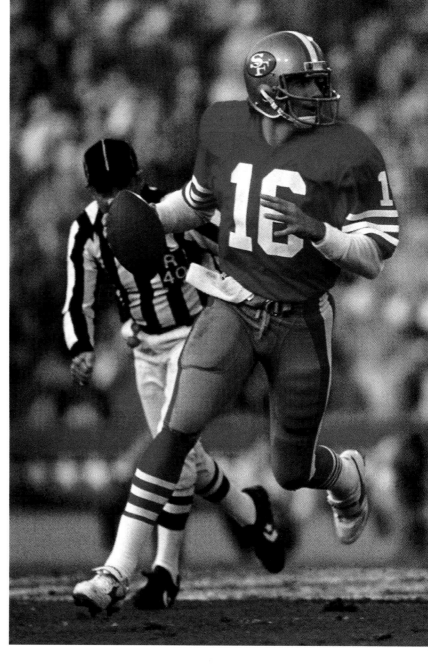

Montana (right) could run if he had to, but he preferred to pass, and his favorite target was Rice (above); the oft-overlooked 49ers defense, led by veteran Ronnie Lott (No. 42, far right) was also critical to San Francisco's dominance in the '80s.

The game was an exciting seesaw affair. The 'Niners struck first on an eight-yard touchdown pass from Montana to Solomon. Later in the first half Montana found one of his favorite targets, wide receiver Dwight Clark, for a 20-yard touchdown. Still, with less than a minute left in the game, the 49ers trailed 27–21. It was time for the first installment of Montana's NFL legend. On third down at the Dallas six-yard line, Montana, under pressure, sprinted to his right and threw the ball high and toward the back of the end zone. Clark used every bit of his 6-foot-

4-inch frame to leap and pull the ball down with his fingertips for the game-winning touchdown. The legend of "The Catch" was born, and the 'Niners were off to the first Super Bowl in franchise history.

Two weeks later they met the Cincinnati Bengals in Super Bowl XVI. Montana passed for one touchdown, ran for another and was named MVP as the 49ers won 26–21. A decade of football dominance had begun in San Francisco.

Three years later, after a 15–1 regular season, the 'Niners reached the Super Bowl again. Now

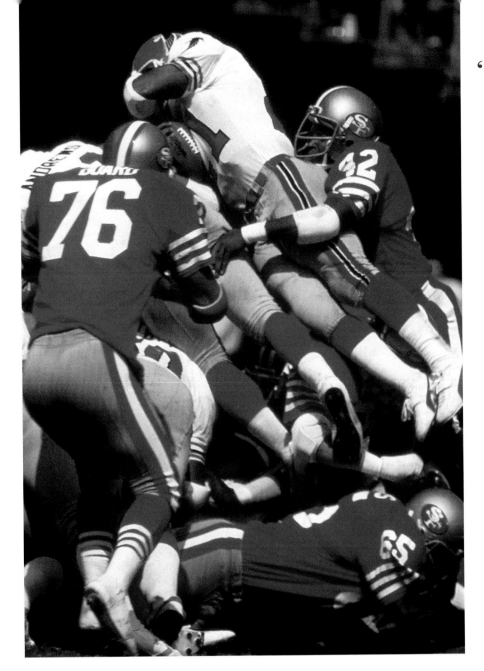

possessing greater balance, San Francisco had two dangerous running backs in the speedy Wendell Tyler and the bruising Roger Craig. The duo took some of the pressure off Montana and the passing game. In their second Super Bowl appearance the 'Niners rolled over young quarterback Dan Marino and the Miami Dolphins 38–16. Montana carved up the Dolphins defense, completing 24 of 35 passes for 331 yards and three touchdowns, and was again named MVP.

The 'Niners made the playoffs the next three years (from 1985 to '87) but failed to advance past

the first round. During those years San Francisco lost players like Clark, Solomon and Tyler to retirement but deftly retooled their offense around new arrivals like the incomparable Jerry Rice, a wide receiver out of tiny Mississippi Valley State. Rice's combination of speed and exceptional hands enabled him to score 16 touchdowns in 1986, and 23 in 1987, a stunning total for a player at any position.

The 49ers won four of their last five games in 1988 to finish at 10–6. They continued their roll in the playoffs as they crushed Minnesota and

Chicago by a combined score of 62–12. They met familiar foe Cincinnati in Super Bowl XXIII in Miami, where Montana was his usual cool self, setting a Super Bowl record with 357 passing yards and engineering a brilliant 11-play, 92-yard drive for the winning touchdown. He zipped a 10-yard pass to wideout John Taylor with 34 seconds remaining to give Walsh and the 'Niners their third Super Bowl victory, 20–16. Rice was named MVP for his record-breaking 215 receiving yards. Walsh retired after the game and was replaced by defensive coordinator George Seifert.

Seifert made a seamless transition, leading the 'Niners to a league-best 14–2 record in 1989. San Francisco steamrolled through the playoffs to make a second straight Super Bowl appearance.

This time, they needed no last-minute heroics from Montana as they crushed John Elway and the Denver Broncos 55–10. Montana threw five touchdown passes. It was the best possible start for the George Seifert era and a fitting conclusion to the '80s, the decade in which the 49ers ruled the NFL.

Few could have predicted the impact Dwight Clark's catch on that January afternoon would have on the 49ers franchise. Clark leaped out of his shoes, and the franchise would follow him. "The Catch" kick-started an era of records and big-game victories that ranks with the best in NFL history. In a city that was renowned for everything but its football team, the 'Niners of the 1980s made watching football on Sunday a real San Francisco treat.

Young (No. 8, opposite) succeeded Montana and led the 49ers into the 1990s, throwing six touchdown passes for Seifert (left) in the 'Niners' Super Bowl XXIX victory over San Diego; Craig (above), a bruising running back who also had great hands, was a key contributor in three of San Francisco's Super Bowl wins.

Aftermath

Though many of their starters' names and faces changed in the 1990s, the 49ers continued their winning ways. After missing the entire 1991 season with an elbow injury and playing only one game in 1992, Joe Montana was traded to the Kansas City Chiefs. He retired in 1994.

Montana's replacement in San Francisco was former USFL quarterback Steve Young, whose arm and mobility made him every bit as scary to defenses as Montana had been. In 1994 the 'Niners bolstered their defense by acquiring linebacker Ken Norton Jr. from Dallas and speedy cornerback Deion Sanders from Atlanta through free agency. They went 13–3 in the regular season and met the San Diego Chargers in Super Bowl XXIX. Young delivered in the big game, throwing a record six touchdown passes and leading San Francisco's 49–26 rout.

George Seifert resigned as 49ers coach in January 1997 and was replaced by former University of California head coach Steve Mariucci. The 1999 season marked the first full season since 1980 that the 'Niners finished with fewer than 10 wins.

COMPACT DISC

Thomas Edison first dragged a stylus through a groove to play recorded sound more than 100 years ago. And while the technology behind Edison's phonograph changed somewhat over time—shellac 78s replaced wax cylinders in the early 1900s, hi-fi long-playing records (LPs) beat out 78s in the '50s and stereo succeeded mono in 1958—the idea remained the same: needle and groove. And with the needle and groove came dust and scratches. And with them, surface noise and skips.

Compact discs, or CDs, eliminated all of the above. They used lasers and microprocessors to produce sound so clear and crisp it was almost indistinguishable from a studio master tape. Invented by Philips and Sony in 1980, these molded aluminum and plastic discs that were only 4.75 inches in diameter hit the U.S. market in 1983. Initially, only audiophiles and classical music lovers were will-

ing to invest $1,000 for a CD player that was of limited usefulness given the paucity of titles available in CD format. (After the medium's first year on the market only 3,500 CD titles were available, compared with some 50,000 LP titles.)

Selling for as much as $20 apiece, CDs were also far more expensive than records and cassette tapes. Many observers predicted they would go the way of quadraphonic sound and 8-track tape players. Record stores hesitated to accord them significant shelf space.

By 1985, though, CDs were single-handedly pulling a listless audio industry out of the doldrums. Players that sold for $1,000 in 1983 could be found for as little as $300, and the price of discs had dropped into the low teens. Demand was so great that customers and stores faced a constant shortage of titles. Record companies couldn't get plants to produce them fast

The growing popularity of the CD (above) prompted stores (left) to devote more and more space to the new medium.

enough. Americans bought 5.8 million CDs in 1984. That number jumped to 22.6 million one year later. As more titles became available—in particular albums by big-selling artists such as the Beatles, Bruce Springsteen and Miles Davis—sales soared. By the end of the decade, Americans were spending some $2 billion on CDs annually.

The CD's biggest selling point was its superior sound quality achieved by digital, as opposed to analog, technology. The audio data on CDs is stored on a reflective metallic layer as minuscule pits (depressions) and lands (flat regions) that spiral out from the disc's center. A laser interprets the pits and lands as a series of binary digits (0s and 1s), which is then converted into sound waves. Errors that occur in the transfer of information are sensed and corrected by the player's computer before the listener picks them up.

This kind of high-tech precision had some musical purists complaining that CD sound was too clinical, even flat or hollow, and that LPs captured the high frequencies better than CDs did. Perhaps, but the CD's tremendous ease of use—pop it in, push a button and let it play for up to 75

minutes—won over the average music listener, who was happy to forget the days of scratches, skips and delicate needles.

Soon players appeared that could hold five CDs at a time and provide more than six hours of uninterrupted play. Using remote control, listeners could choose the order of discs and songs, replay a favorite tune or skip one without ever leaving their chairs. CDs, with their slim .05-inch profile, were also highly portable—the Discman premiered in 1984—and seemingly indestructible. The laser, which reads the binary code, never physically touches the laminated surface of the CD, so the disc isn't subject to the kind of wear and tear that affects albums and tapes.

Because CDs could store text and graphics as well as music, they had applications far beyond the audio industry and spawned a virtual alphabet of CD-based applications: CD-ROM (Read Only Memory), CD-I (Interactive), DVI (Digital Video Interactive), CDTV (Commodore Dynamic Total Vision), CD-R (Recordable), Thor-CD (erasable CD), CDV (Video) and DVD (Digital Video Disc).

To hear why Genesis records on Sony digital equipment, play them back on a Sony Compact Disc Player.

When it comes to capturing the experience of live music, no audio equipment delivers the lifelike reproduction of digital audio.

That's why the only digital recording equipment chosen by Tony Banks, Phil Collins and Mike Rutherford of Genesis is, not surprisingly, the leader in the industry: Sony.

Not only has Sony led the way in professional digital recording equipment, we invented the digital audio system for play-

So why not do what Genesis does? Play back the top-selling compact discs like "Invisible Touch" the way they were mastered. On Sony Digital equipment. You'll find that when it comes to bringing you close to the music, nothing even comes close.

The Sony CDP-55. Sony's best value in a full-featured compact disc player.

From its Unilinear Converter and digital filter to its programming flexibility and supplied Remote Commander* unit, the Sony CDP-55 has everything you need in a home CD player.

SONY. THE LEADER IN DIGITAL AUDIO™

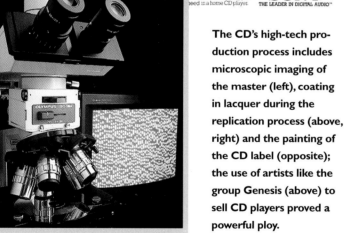

The CD's high-tech production process includes microscopic imaging of the master (left), coating in lacquer during the replication process (above, right) and the painting of the CD label (opposite); the use of artists like the group Genesis (above) to sell CD players proved a powerful ploy.

"Long playing records will be a footnote in history 10 years from now."

—KEN POHLMANN,
CD expert and author, 1986

Aftermath

In 1997 alone, consumers who by then had largely replaced their old vinyl collections spent $750 million on CDs. Great hopes for the new MiniDisc systems that use three-inch CDs had not been met by century's end, but after 16 years in the making, new CD-Rs (Recordables) were set to capture mass-market appeal as a recording medium. Downloadable sound files called MP3s and MP4s, another potentially successful format, became available on the Internet in the late '90s.

Some lasted, some did not. In any case, the electronics industry was forever altered. Take the CD-ROM, for instance. One CD-ROM could hold an entire set of encylopedias, not to mention massive amounts of computer programming. It would take hundreds of floppy disks to store the more than 600 megabytes of data accommodated by one CD-ROM. They were perfect for handling games and software. Within a decade CD-ROM drives would be a standard feature on computers.

The jury was still out on whether LPs or CDs offered superior sound quality, but compact disc technology was clearly here to stay. By mid-decade some classical music labels were issuing titles only on CD. Tower Records was devoting less than one-third of its space to LPs by 1989, down from 60 percent in 1985. And mega-retailers like K-Mart and Target had dropped vinyl altogether.

CABBAGE PATCH KIDS

The holiday season is a time for peace, kindness and goodwill toward men. But in 1983 the seasonal spirit showed its darker side as millions of parents shoved and screamed for the right to pay as much as $150 for an ugly, runt-of-the-litter doll called a Cabbage Patch Kid.

In shopping malls across the country, mature, seemingly normal adults were transformed into frantic lunatics who feared their children would be the only kids on the block without the coveted doll. Some parents waited in line for as long as 14 hours to buy a Cabbage Patch Kid. Angry words were exchanged, department store managers threatened. In Wilkes-Barre, Pennsylvania, a woman broke her leg when a swarm of 1,000 people became violent after eight hours of waiting. The store manager was forced to defend himself with a baseball bat. "It's like watching a football game," said the manager of a South Carolina

department store after he witnessed 50 people scramble for a half dozen Kids. Not everyone, though, was willing to wait in line. A Kansas City postman flew to London for the sole purpose of buying a Kid for his five-year-old daughter.

This aberrant behavior was even more puzzling once you saw what everyone was fighting over. The Kids all had faces only a mother could love. Offering unconditional love, the Cabbage Patch Kids were marketed with birth certificates and their own adoption papers. Kids, therefore, weren't purchased, they were adopted—for a fee, of course.

In an age dominated by electronic toys, the Cabbage Patch Kid was not the typical 1980s hot-seller. It couldn't speak, it couldn't walk, it didn't even wet its pants. What made it unique was that it *was* unique. Coleco, which licensed the dolls from Original Appalachian Artworks,

The doll with a face only a mother could love (left) inspired buying frenzies across the country (above).

sold nearly three million of them in 1983, and no two were identical. By varying hair color, dimples, freckles and other characteristics, the dolls' creators succeeded in making each "parent" feel as if his or her Kid were special.

Coleco's clever marketing of Cabbage Patch Kids as one-of-a-kind toddlers appealed immensely to young children. Imagining that they are adopted is a natural fantasy for children, and Kids offered them an opportunity to act out that fantasy in a healthful way. The sheer homeliness of the doll also worked in its favor. "It is

comforting," wrote popular psychologist Dr. Joyce Brothers, "to feel the Cabbage Patch doll can be loved with all your might—even though it isn't pretty."

But children weren't the only fans of Kids. A 60-year-old grandmother from Georgia owned more than 40 of the dolls and spent a large part of her time dressing and caring for them. A New Jersey man hosted Camp Small Fry, a four- or eight-week summer camp just for Cabbage Patch Kids that offered a photograph of each Kid with his or her bunkmates, a camp T-shirt and a letter

"They knocked over the display table. People were grabbing at each other, pushing and shoving. It got ugly."

—Scott Belcher, a toy store manager in West Virginia, after witnessing a Cabbage Patch Kid frenzy

A veritable explosion of Cabbage Patch Kids (left) was needed to keep up with the national craze that brought intensive media coverage (inset) to the companionable doll (far right) created by Xavier Roberts (above).

home each week. More than 50 Kids signed up.

The overwhelming demand for the dolls took everyone by surprise, including the Kids' creator, Xavier Roberts. "I'm just amazed," he said in 1983. "Sometimes, I just stand there watching, and no one knows that I'm the one who started it all."

Roberts was a 21-year-old art student in 1976 when he began making his unique batch of dolls, which he called Little People. He devised the hokey ritual of adoption—dolls were not made, but "delivered," and his employees wore white nurse's uniforms. Robert's dressed his 22-inch creations in secondhand children's clothing from yard sales and gave them individual names chosen from a 1937 Georgia birth registry.

His handcrafted dolls quickly grew in popularity, especially among adults, who bought them at arts and crafts shows across the Southeast. In 1981 it was reported that early editions of Roberts's Little People were being "re-adopted" for as much as 25 times their initial $40 "adoption" fee. The following year, Roberts negotiated a deal with Coleco to mass-produce a smaller, 16-inch version of his doll with a vinyl head and soft body, which sold for $25.

By Thanksgiving 1983, 15 months after Roberts signed with Coleco, retail inventories of the new version of the doll were depleted and panic ensued. Cabbage Patch Kids went on record as the most successful new doll in the history of the toy industry.

Part of the Cabbage Patch appeal was each doll's uniqueness (left, top, and opposite bottom), attested to by birth certificates and adoption papers (right). Empty store shelves (opposite) spelled disappointment for those who looked foward to picking out clothes for a new Kid (above).

Aftermath

Cabbage Patch Kids continued to fly off the shelves after Christmas 1983. In 1985 Coleco racked up $600 million in Kids sales. The dolls remained popular, but in 1988 Coleco filed for bankruptcy. Mattel assumed the manufacturing and marketing of the dolls in 1995, and Cabbage Patch Kids remained one of the best-selling toys of all time. From 1983 to '99, more than 95 million Kids were "adopted" worldwide.

HOSTAGES COME HOME

On November 4, 1979, a rainy Sunday in Teheran, hundreds of radical Muslim students scaled the walls and broke through the iron gates of the sprawling United States embassy compound, shouting *Marg bar Amrika,* "Death to America." President Jimmy Carter had just let Iran's exiled monarch, Shah Mohammad Reza Pahlavi, enter the United States to seek medical treatment, and in so doing he infuriated Iran's growing fundamentalist factions who felt the shah should be returned to Iran to stand trial.

Hostages Come Home

33 USA

The student militants took 66 embassy employees captive, a move that was sanctioned by religious revolutionary Ayatollah Ruhollah Khomeini, whose theocracy would soon replace Iran's provisional government. Thirteen women and "oppressed" African-American hostages were released within two weeks of their capture, but the remaining 53 (one hostage would be released after 245 days due to illness) representatives of "the Great Satan" would suffer through 444 days of captivity that nearly brought one of the world's superpowers to its knees.

A critical observer might say that the United States should have seen it coming. In 1953 the CIA backed the coup that brought the shah to power in order to secure U.S. access to Iranian oil and to counterbalance Soviet influence in the Middle East. Successive administrations nurtured the relationship by facilitating industrialization, supplying arms and turning a blind eye to the shah's increasingly repressive regime—a monarchy which, among other things, confiscated vast land holdings from Muslim clerics, stole from the nation's oil-rich tills and deployed a vicious secret police to squelch dissent from religious fundamentalists like Khomeini. The majority of Iranians, however, did not embrace the materialism,

From ticker tape in New York City (left) to yellow ribbons in D.C. (above), the hostages received a hero's homecoming.

The images from Iran were less than reassuring: the American flag being burned as onlookers cheered (above); a horde of pro-Khomeini demonstrators in Teheran (right); wreckage from the aborted rescue mission (opposite, top); and a blindfolded hostage (opposite, bottom) being paraded by Iranian captors.

secularization and emancipation of women that rapid modernization brought. In hindsight it seemed like only a matter of time before Iran forged a response.

From the moment the embassy was seized, images from Teheran dominated the U.S. nightly news: blindfolded hostages—their hands bound with tape—being paraded across the embassy grounds; Iranians setting fire to American flags; effigies of President Carter and the shah engulfed in flames; and placards bearing the steely eyes of Ayatollah Khomeini being hoisted above frenzied crowds. The mighty U.S. was shaken and humiliated by a small desert nation, and with each passing day of the hostages' captivity somberly noted on the evening news, the nation became increasingly demoralized.

Inspired by the pop song "Tie a Yellow Ribbon 'Round the Old Oak Tree," Americans from Seattle to Sarasota tied yellow ribbons around trees, tele-

"We've had a change of presidency, but even that was second in people's minds."

—*JIMMY CARTER, February 2, 1981*

phone poles and porches in solidarity with the prisoners. It seemed to be about as much as anyone could do. The captors' threats to "destroy all the hostages immediately" if provoked made retaliation unthinkable, and the Ayatollah's Byzantine government offered little hope for meaningful negotiations.

Pentagon officials, however, envisioned a third course of action—a daring rescue mission they began planning the day the hostages were taken. If Operation Eagle Claw succeeded, Carter would be a

hero. As it was, the mission, launched on the 170th day of the crisis, came to a disastrous end. Two U.S. aircraft collided after the decision to abort due to logistical problems had been made. Eight servicemen died in the Iranian desert. The national psyche, and Carter's flagging popularity, hit bottom.

Then, in an odd twist of fate, Iraq extended a helping hand to the United States when it invaded Iran on September 22, 1980. To fight its neighbor, Iran would need the billions of dollars that Carter

71

had ordered frozen by U.S. banks at the beginning of the hostage crisis. Iran would also need parts for its U.S.-supplied weapons. Suddenly, the Ayatollah had reason to negotiate. He wasted little time. On November 2, 1980, just two days before U.S. voters went to the polls to choose their 40th president, Carter received an agreement from Iran to free the hostages. His campaign sorely needed good news: Inflation and unemployment were both in double digits, oil prices were soaring and interest rates were at an all-time high. Cautiously, Carter steered clear of announcing a breakthrough in the hostage crisis, informing the country instead of a "constructive step" in the negotiations that were being mediated by Algeria. He lost the election by a landslide to the charismatic actor-turned-politician Ronald Reagan.

In the remaining months of Carter's administration, the U.S. team of negotiators, lead by Assistant Secretary of State Warren Christopher, worked feverishly on a complex deal they hoped would free the captives before Carter left office. At 8 a.m. on January 20, 1981, the day of Reagan's swearing in, Carter received word that $8 billion in Iranian assets had been released in what likely ranks as the largest private transfer of funds in history. At 12:33 p.m. EST, 11 minutes after Reagan's inauguration and 444 days after the crisis began, the first plane carrying hostages departed Teheran toward freedom. The nightmare had ended, and the country began its jubilant passage into the new decade of conspicuous consumption and unbridled optimism.

After they left Iranian soil, the hostages were flown first to the U.S. Air Force base in Frankfurt, West Germany, where David Roeder deplaned jubilantly (above); they then continued on to warm embraces at Andrews Air Force Base in Maryland (left) and crowds of well-wishers in Washington, D.C. (opposite).

Aftermath

Although Iran suffered net diplomatic and financial losses from the hostage crisis, the siege set the stage for future acts of terrorism and hostage-taking in the '80s. At the beginning of Reagan's first term in office Americans were kidnapped in war-torn Lebanon. Claiming that negotiation with terrorists only encouraged them, Reagan publicly refused to engage in dialogue with the new captors. But privately, he sanctioned what would become known as the Iran-Contra scandal: a covert deal in which the United States would illegally sell arms to Iran, who would in turn apply pressure to the kidnappers. The proceeds from the arms sales would then be illegally funneled to the Contras, anti-Sandinista rebels in Nicaragua.

When the story broke, a special prosecutor was named and hearings were held. Despite overwhelming evidence against his administration, Reagan emerged relatively unscathed, and nobody involved in the scandal spent time in prison.

CATS

Throughout the summer of 1982 ominous black banners trailed airplanes in the heat-saturated air above New York City, slanted yellow eyes stared intensely from newspaper ads and signs the size of buildings bore the cryptic message, "*Cats* is Coming…"

When *Cats* opened to great expectations at Broadway's Winter Garden Theater on October 7, critical response was mixed. The show had been a smash in London, but New York, mecca of the musical, was different. Few could predict how Americans would respond to an unorthodox British musical devoid of plot and starring 26 clawing, mewling and hissing humanoid felines with names like Grizabella, Skimbleshanks, Old Deuteronomy and Bustopher Jones. Audiences were dazzled.

It might have been all "sound and furry" as one critic reported, but at least, conceded most, it was different from the star-driven and formulaic musicals that characterized Broadway in the early '80s. A dance marathon from beginning to end, *Cats* was sheer spectacle with Spielbergian pyrotechnics—and a budget to match (U.S. producers spent $4.5 million before opening night).

The musical had its origins in T. S. Eliot's book of light verse, originally written for his godchild and published in 1939 as *Old Possum's Book of Practical Cats*. As a young boy, composer Andrew Lloyd Webber had been delighted by the lyrical poems in Eliot's book and in 1977—with successful musicals such as *Jesus Christ Superstar* and *Evita* under his belt—he began composing a song cycle. After Eliot's widow unexpectedly produced unfinished feline-inspired poems, Webber envisioned staging a full-scale musical. "We are going to build a whole cat-world environment," he said. "They will climb over the audience. They will fly."

Designer John Napier fulfilled Webber's wishes, creating a magical feline fantasy world. As theatergoers settled in, the hall darkened and hundreds of

By decade's end the mewling cast of *Cats* (left) had lured millions of theatergoers to the Winter Garden (above).

CATS™ © 1981 RUG ltd.

"There is no limit to what cats can do with their bodies, if you watch."

—*GILLIAN LYNNE, choreographer of* Cats

Napier's elaborate costumes (Rum Tum Tugger, top, Jennyanydots, far left, Bombalurina, left) and Webber's inspired music for a chorus of 26 cats (opposite) brought T. S. Eliot's book of poems (inset) to life.

fluorescent cat's eyes stared out from the blackness. Webber's 25-piece orchestra thundered. Strobe lights pierced the darkness, illuminating a probing paw here, a coiling tail there. Thousands of casually draped Christmas tree lights sputtered on as tigers, toms and tabbies climbed furtively through a giant junkyard that spilled messily over the stage, across the balconies and up to the rafters. Oversized bicycles, ancient car tires, discarded Christmas decorations, a decrepit car littered the stage—all props for the frolicking felines.

In the months before the London opening, choreographer Gillian Lynne had worked with a team of actors to develop an anthology of feline mannerisms. At open auditions in New York City, she urged the hundreds of hopefuls to find a new, capricious energy, "Darlings, imagine it is 3 a.m., somewhere strange like Stonehenge, a place where cats congregate. I want you each to be a cat who likes elegance and mystique. Roll your hips, massage your thighs . . ."

While the cats onstage were all clearly of the same slinking species, they were quite different from one another in temperament. Director Trevor Nunn worked with the actors to create highly nuanced felines. Take Rum Tum Tugger, the wild,

bad-boy rock star tomcat whose cheeky, ornery independence delighted audiences. Or the cozy, matronly old Gumbie cat named Jennyanydots, who sat in the sun by day and kept mice and cockroaches under her paws by night: "She is deeply concerned with the ways of the mice/Their behavior's not good and their manners not nice." Bustopher Jones, the elegant about-town aesthete, sported a cane and a monstrous bulk, "He's the Cat we all greet as he walks down the street in his coat of fastidious black." Of Growltiger the barge cat, known as "the Terror of the Thames," they sang, "One ear was somewhat missing, no need to tell you why/And he scowled upon a hostile world from one forbidding eye." But the queen of kitty pathos was the bedraggled, erstwhile glamour puss, Grizabella, who sings of her fall from grace in "Memory," a song that became a hit even before its Broadway debut.

Whatever the theater critics said, nobody could deny that by the end of the decade, *Cats* had firmly nestled itself in the crook of America's arm. It had become the most lucrative theatrical venture of all time and had joined New York City's ranks of "must see" tourist attractions.

Spectacular set design (left) and the catlike gestures of the actors (above and below) transported *Cats* audiences to a dazzling world of feline fantasy.

Aftermath

On June 19, 1997, *Cats* celebrated its 6,138th performance and, after 15 years of unabated popularity, superseded *A Chorus Line* as the longest-running Broadway musical ever. More than 235 actors have donned the feline gear since opening night in 1981, and Grizabella's lament, "Memory," has been recorded by more than 150 singers, including Barbra Streisand, Barry Manilow and Judy Collins. The musical has become a veritable cash cow (or cat), having played in more than 20 countries to more than 50 million people and grossed $2 billion worldwide.

CABLE TV

It was June 1, 1980, and whatever doubts they may have once had on the subject, everybody in the world of television was now certain that Ted Turner was out of his mind. Once dubbed the "Mouth of the South" by *Time* magazine, Turner had always been regarded as a bit of a wild man, but he was also widely admired as a shrewd, visionary businessman who had built a small television and pro sports empire upon the ashes of his father's billboard business in Atlanta.

But now it looked as if Turner's soaring success had made him dizzy. He had mortgaged every business he owned to finance a cable channel called Cable News Network, or CNN. It would broadcast 24 hours a day using raw news footage and bargain basement on-air talent. What it lacked in sophistication, it planned to make up for in thoroughness and availability. The six o'clock news, whenever you wanted it! Still, it seemed risky to take on all three established networks, and even

Turner's admirers believed that CNN would give him his comeuppance. Certainly the omens weren't good: ESPN, the new round-the-clock sports network that had been launched in '79, was losing so much money its owners were contemplating the heretical step of charging a monthly fee.

In its first year CNN lost $20 million, forcing Turner to borrow $200 million. When ABC and Westinghouse teamed up to start their own all-news network, CNN's demise seemed certain. But not so. In its second year Turner's folly broke even, reaching 10 million subscribers.

Cable technology actually developed in the late 1940s, and its early history was the story of men very much like Turner: hungry entrepreneurs who, with nothing to lose in a booming postwar economy, saw a tremendous opportunity in the miracle of television and leaped at it. Ever since RCA introduced television at the 1939 World's Fair, the new

Fiberoptic cables (left) carried cable networks such as CNN (above) to more than 50 million households by decade's end.

technology's biggest obstacle was the fact that, unlike radio waves, which bounce off the atmosphere and ricochet off impediments, television signals travel in a straight line and stop when they meet an obstacle such as a mountain. As a result, early television stations had a limited range and equally limited advertising revenues. Industry pioneers used cable to solve this problem.

Most of the early systems were in rural areas, especially in the West, where there were few places populated enough to support their own television station and mountains that prevented signals from traveling very far. In Casper, Wyoming, for example, a former fighter pilot and boxer named Bill Daniels took a signal from Laramie, 150 miles to the south, and relayed it to Casper, where it was then delivered to homes by cables for a $150 installation fee and a subscription of $7.50 per month. With no other entertainment for miles around, nobody balked at

the price, or at the fact that it was only available for eight hours a day. "They really didn't care what it cost," said Gene Schneider, an engineer who constructed the system for Daniels. "We were just signing up people to subscribe like crazy."

In its infancy, cable was a largely unregulated industry. But in 1968 the U.S. Supreme Court ruled 7–0 in *U.S. v. Southwestern Cable Company* that the FCC had the authority to regulate it, which it proceeded to do with rules that slowed growth. That changed again in the late '70s when a new FCC chairman, Charles Ferris, took a more benign view of the industry. In July 1980, one month after Turner launched CNN, the FCC repealed most of the restrictive legislation that had been passed in the '60s and '70s. In 1984 Congress passed the Cable Communications Policy Act (CCPA), which transferred power from states and cities to the federal government but essen-

> ## "I couldn't get it out of my mind. How do you get that great invention to a small town that didn't have any television stations?"
>
> —*BILL DANIELS,*
> *recalling what drove him to begin*
> *the development of cable television*

Cable television offered a diverse programming menu that included music videos on MTV (opposite), live, unfiltered coverage of Senate and House proceedings on C-SPAN (left) and round-the-clock sports broadcasting on ESPN (below); CNN's nonstop coverage of the Gulf War made reporter Peter Arnett (inset) a familiar face to millions of Americans.

tially lifted many of the restrictions the cable industry had complained about.

In the 1980s the industry more than doubled in size, from 14.8 million subscribers in 1979 to 52.5 million in '89. Music Television (MTV) made its debut in 1981; The Weather Channel and CNN Headline News in 1982; The Nashville Network (TNN) in 1983; Lifetime Television in 1984 and the Home Shopping Network in 1985. With that, most of what we now think of as the basic "package" of cable programming was in place. By 1991, after more than 10 years of astounding growth in the cable industry, ESPN had become the most popular cable station and Ted Turner, the Mouth of the South, was named *Time*'s Man of the Year.

Peter Arnett
Baghdad, Iraq
CNN

Aftermath

Though cable reached 67 percent of homes in America in 1999, the time seemed ripe for Direct To Home (DTH) and Direct Broadcast Satellite (DBS) systems. The former was tried in the early 1980s but failed for a number of reasons, including its expense and the scarcity of available channels. But in the late '90s mass-produced satellite dishes that were small enough to go virtually unnoticed and cost just $200 were widely available. Add to that superior picture quality and a wealth of programming options, and it was no wonder that in 1998 there were 5 million DBS subscribers.

HIP-HOP CULTURE

What you hear is not a test
I'm rappin' to the beat
And me, the groove and my friends
Are going to try to move your feet.

"Rapper's Delight" probably did sound a lot like a microphone test to those first encountering its giddy street rhymes in October 1979. What they were hearing was a catchy hodgepodge of playground boasts, nonsense verse and a kind of "scat speaking," all of it "rapped" by the Sugar Hill Gang's three MCs over an infectious guitar riff bor-rowed from the Chic song, "Good Times." As music it was literally someone else's; as poetry it was crude and sophomoric. But what "Rapper's Delight" lacked in sophistication it made up for in exuberance. And in its celebration of ego and materialism, it was the perfect fanfare for the '80s, a decade in which President Ronald Reagan gave his avuncular blessing to

self-interest, and rap music defied all predictions of its imminent demise to become the most successful and controversial of all popular musical styles.

Twenty years later, when rap had become such a convenient cultural boogeyman, it was difficult to remember that in the beginning it was party music, plain and simple. A DJ's fondest wish was to keep the dance floor moving and maybe even to get the celebrants to throw their hands in the air and wave them like they just didn't care.

Unlike disco, which was expiring at the end of the '70s, hip-hop had humble roots. It bubbled up from the crumbling streets of the Bronx, where in the late '70s turntable wizards like Kool Herc, Afrika Bambaataa and Grandmaster Flash drew huge crowds by dragging their booming sound systems into schoolyards, roller rinks and small clubs and playing funk records they had scavenged at used record stores. A key part of Herc's show was the vocal ad libs of his

Graffiti, break dancing (left), rap music and boom boxes (above) were the four cornerstones of hip-hop culture.

85

Requiring no more than a patch of pavement and a beat, a break dancer turns a Los Angeles sidewalk into a stage (right); the movie *Beat Street* (lower left) brought hip-hop from the street corner to the big screen.

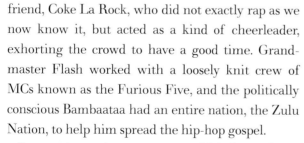

Hip-hop artists Afrika Bambaataa (inset above), Grandmaster Flash (inset right) and Run DMC (top, left) fused turntable wizardry and rapid-fire lyrics to create rap music.

friend, Coke La Rock, who did not exactly rap as we now know it, but acted as a kind of cheerleader, exhorting the crowd to have a good time. Grandmaster Flash worked with a loosely knit crew of MCs known as the Furious Five, and the politically conscious Bambaataa had an entire nation, the Zulu Nation, to help him spread the hip-hop gospel.

But music was just one aspect of hip-hop culture. Just as important were the acrobatic dance style, known as breaking, and graffiti writing, or "tagging" as its practitioners called it. In the early '80s it seemed as if every corner of Manhattan was a hip-hop party.

Every sidewalk had a crew of lithe break dancers spinning on their heads, and taggers got their kicks sneaking into subway railyards at night armed with cans of Krylon and Red Devil spray paint and then watching their fantastically lettered canvases speed around the city. At one level, hip-hop was about marking territory, claiming space and insisting to an America intoxicated by profit, "We live here too!"

In 1982 Grandmaster Flash commented on the

Reagan era with "The Message," a hip-hop masterpiece that took listeners on a grim snapshot tour of the ghetto and left them with an ominous warning: "Don't push me 'cause I'm close to the edge/I'm tryin' not to lose my head." It is amazing in retrospect to realize how conservative "The Message" actually is: antidrug and proeducation and self-respect.

Hip-hop had many critics, from conservative observers like William Bennett and C. Delores Tucker to mayors bent on stamping out graffiti and musicians who said that what little was good about rap came from borrowed—or "sampled"—sources.

"**Like the graffiti writers and the break dancers, the old school DJs, and those that quickly followed their lead, did it because it felt good and because they could.**"

—*NELSON GEORGE, hip-hop historian, 1998*

"Rap?" sneered rocker Gregg Allman. "Short for crap." To many, rap seemed irresponsible or frightening—theme music for crack-dealing black teens. As proof, they needed to look no further than *Straight Outta Compton* by N.W.A. (Niggaz With Attitude), which included the incendiary "F*** Tha Police."

But the truth about hip-hop was always more complicated than its enemies would allow. For every "gangsta" rapper, there were others like Queen Latifah, the literal embodiment of powerful African-American women. Hip-hop music may have set back the cause of good spelling, but it spoke in many voices, from Public Enemy's uncompromising black nationalism to the Beastie Boys' heavy-metal-driven party music. The biggest sellers were Run D.M.C., from Hollis, Queens. They

teamed up with the rock band Aerosmith on "Walk This Way," which reached No. 4 on the charts and helped the album it was on, *Raising Hell,* become the first hip-hop album to go platinum.

By the end of the decade, there was no question that hip-hop music was here to stay. It got its first TV show, *Yo, MTV Raps!,* in 1988, the same year it got its first magazine, *Source.* In 1989 it became New York City policy to pull all graffiti-tagged cars out of service until they could be cleaned, but by then the music had become about as mainstream as possible. MC Hammer's "U Can't Touch This," released in 1990, sold 10 million copies, while much maligned white rapper Vanilla Ice's "Ice Ice Baby" became the first rap to hit No. 1. Like it or not, hip-hop had become as American as apple pie.

To hip-hop detractors, **Public Enemy** was more than just the name of a rap band (below), it was how they perceived the youths who tagged subway cars (above and inset) and danced explosively to blaring boom boxes (opposite).

Aftermath

Though it has managed to keep most subway cars graffiti-free since 1989, the city of New York had to spend $25 million in 1998 alone to do so. There is a Graffiti Hall of Fame on a wall at the corner of 106th Street and Park Avenue in Harlem, but taggers of the 1990s, like their forebears, preferred to use less sanctioned walls, especially in the face of Mayor Rudy Giuliani's "quality of life" campaign in New York City. Late-century taggers concentrated on subway tunnels, storefront grates, billboards and the streets themselves. Said gallery owner Hugo Martinez, "These kids want to establish a new way of doing things, a new way of looking at identity and property. They want to redefine the world so that their name is on it."

SPACE SHUTTLE PROGRAM

When NASA's Apollo program concluded at the end of the 1960s, the question on the lips of the scientific community and the public at large was, "What do we do next in manned space?" According to Dr. Milton Silveira, NASA's chief engineer during the mid-1980s, the space shuttle provided the answer to that question.

The shuttle opened a new era in the space age: With its development, astronauts could not only launch satellites and exploratory craft into orbit, they could also set up shop, as it were, in space. A controlled and relatively roomy environment, the shuttle allowed its occupants to conduct experiments, retrieve and repair craft already in orbit and observe the Earth and the solar system from a revolutionary vantage point. The shuttle also allowed longer stays in space than had ever been attempted before and yielded valuable data about the effects of such prolonged tours of space on human beings. The

next step in manned space, the space shuttle was a giant leap forward in mankind's quest to explore the heavens.

In development since the early '70s, the first space shuttle, *Columbia*, was launched on April 12, 1981. The first of four "test flights" over a 15-month period, its mission was to demonstrate that an airplanelike manned spacecraft could be launched into orbit and returned to Earth safely. John W. Young and Robert L. Crippen were the astronauts on board, and 12 minutes after takeoff, they entered the Earth's orbit, 175 statute miles above the planet.

During their voyage, Young and Crippen beamed pictures back to Earth, one of which revealed that the shuttle had lost several heat-shielding tiles in the cargo bay. This was deemed a minor loss, and the remaining 30,000-plus tiles held firm as the shuttle braved the 3,000°F temperature during reentry to Earth's atmosphere.

Atlantis **(left, clearing the launch tower) and** *Discovery* **(above, touching down) made up half of NASA's shuttle fleet.**

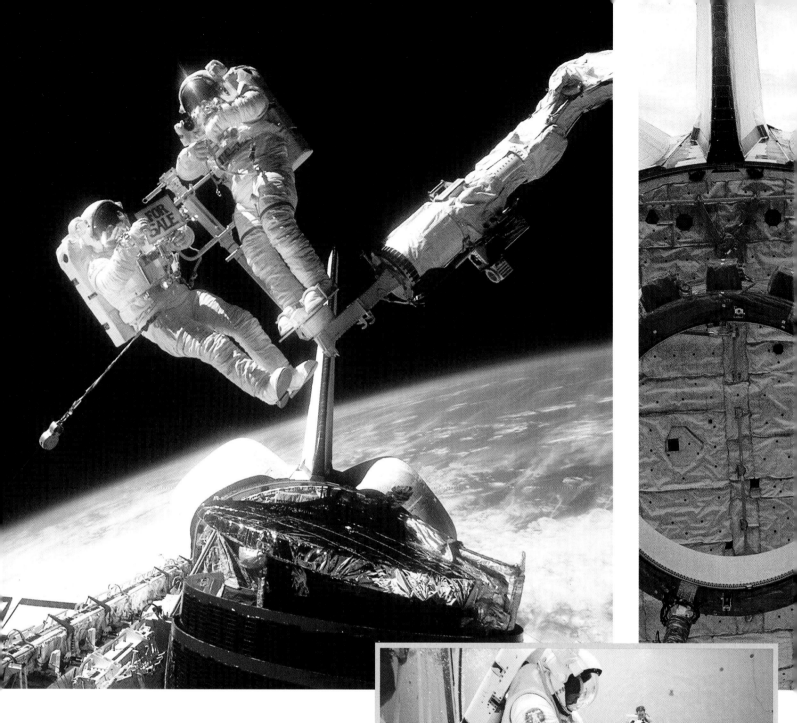

Astronaut Story Musgrave orbited cloud-shrouded Earth in *Challenger*'s cargo bay (opposite); Astronauts James D. van Hoften and George D. Nelson (inset, left and right, respectively) trained underwater in Johnson Space Center's weightless environment facility; astronauts Dale A. Gardner and Joseph P. Allen (above, left and right, respectively) recaptured a stranded communications spacecraft and jokingly offered it up "for sale."

After 2 days, 6 hours and 20 minutes, Crippen and Young brought *Columbia* in for a picture-perfect landing in the bed of Rogers Dry Lake in California's Mojave Desert. The astronauts had orbited the earth 36 times and traveled 933,757 miles. "What a way to come to California!" said Crippen.

Columbia would complete five successful journeys, including the first operational flight, which deployed two commercial communications satel-lites, before ceding the launch pad to its successor, *Challenger*, in April 1983.

On *Challenger*'s first mission, two members of its four-man crew, Donald Peterson and Story Musgrave, became the 28th and 29th Americans to walk in space, and on the ship's second flight, in June 1983, Sally Ride became the first American woman ever to fly into space. Tragically, *Challenger* is best known though for its tenth flight: the only fatal mission in the space shuttle program's history.

On January 28, 1986, *Challenger* exploded in the air above Cape Canaveral, Florida, 73 seconds after liftoff. All seven crew members were killed. The disaster was witnessed by thousands of people on the ground at the Kennedy Space Center and millions watching it on live television. Deepening the nation's sense of tragedy was the presence on *Challenger* of Christa McAuliffe, a schoolteacher and mother of two from Concord, New Hampshire, who was to be the first ordinary citizen in space as part of NASA's "Teacher-in-Space" program.

The government's Rogers Commission, which included Nobel Prize-winning physicist Richard Feynman, traced the disaster to the failure of the O-rings, a set of gaskets in the rocket boosters. The O-rings froze and weakened in the cold

Crew members advertised their successful satellite deployment (above); the first American woman in space, Sally Ride, cleaned an air-filtering system on board *Challenger* (inset); **the crew of the ill-fated *Challenger* mission 51-L was photographed on its way to the shuttle (opposite), which exploded just 73 seconds into its flight (opposite, inset).**

weather that day, releasing a flame that touched off the explosion in the rocket's main fuel tank. The commission criticized NASA for launching the shuttle in the unusually cold temperature and for its safety standards in general.

After the fateful *Challenger* mission—the 25th space shuttle flight—the program was grounded for 32 months while NASA made more than 400 modifications to its four ships. The first post-*Challenger* mission lifted off on September 29, 1988, when the shuttle *Discovery* took five crew members up into orbit and deployed a $100 million Tracking and Data Relay Satellite.

The shuttle program was operational throughout the 1990s, and while flights were not quite routine, NASA successfully launched about six missions per year, ushering the era of manned space into the new millennium.

Aftermath

From September 1988, when it reopened the space shuttle program, to August '99, NASA launched 70 successful flights of its four crafts, *Columbia, Discovery, Atlantis* and *Endeavour*, which replaced *Challenger*.

On October 29, 1998, former astronaut John Glenn, 77, became the oldest person ever to travel in space when he blasted off in *Discovery*. In 1962, Glenn had been the first American ever to orbit the Earth.

The shuttle program achieved another milestone on July 27, 1999, when Eileen Collins became the first woman ever to pilot a U.S. space flight. Collins commanded *Columbia* on a five-day mission to deploy the $1.5 billion telescope *Chandra.* "This is an absolutely tremendous day for science," said Roger Brissenden, manager of *Chandra*'s control center. "The most exciting part for me is the discoveries *Chandra* will make that we don't yet know about."

INDEX